The
POOH
CORNER
COOK BOOK

The
POOH
CORNER
COOK BOOK

Inspired by
WINNIE-THE-POOH
and
THE HOUSE AT POOH CORNER
by A. A. Milne

Recipes by KATIE STEWART
Illustrated by ERNEST SHEPARD

Methuen Children's Books · London

First published in Great Britain 1980 by Methuen Children's Books Ltd
11 New Fetter Lane, London EC4
Individual copyright for text and illustrations:
Winnie-the-Pooh copyright 1926
The House at Pooh Corner copyright 1928
Recipes © 1980 Katie Stewart
All rights reserved
Filmset, printed and bound in Great Britain by
Hazell Watson & Viney Ltd, Aylesbury

ISBN 0 416 88310 9

British Library Cataloguing in Publication Data

Stewart, Katie
The Pooh Corner cook book.
1. Cookery – Juvenile literature
I. Title
641.5   TX652.5

ISBN 0 416 88310 9

Contents

Piglet – snack and supper things

Rabbit – salads and health foods

Tigger – picnic and 'expotition' foods

Kanga and Roo – puddings

Christopher Robin – cold drinks and ices

Eeyore – soups and vegetable dishes

The recipes which are marked * are the easiest to make

Introduction

Here is a cookery book from Pooh and his friends with recipes specially chosen for you to make. You will find there are all kinds of ideas that you will enjoy cooking up for your friends and family — with Pooh you can make some sweets that will make welcome presents, or bake his favourite honey nut bread; you can cook some of Piglet's suggestions for snack and supper things, or Tigger's good ideas that you will find ideal for picnics and when you feel like a cool drink or a home made ice cream, then Christopher Robin can help. These recipes will give you hours of fun and pleasure.

Each recipe has a quotation from the Winnie-the-Pooh stories and there are lots of the lovely drawings by Ernest Shepard. You can have fun identifying the characters and guessing from which story the quotations come. No one ever tires of reading the amusing adventures of Pooh and his friends and if it's ages since you read them, then you should try reading them again and it will add even more interest to the recipes as you cook.

You will find cooking fun and very rewarding. If you have never tried before, look for the easy recipes and make them first — a * indicates them for you on the contents page. Look through the list of helpful hints before you start and when you turn to the recipes you will find that everything has been set down very clearly so that they are easy to understand. Follow the recipes carefully and the results will be delicious.

Helpful hints

Read the recipe through before you start to make sure you have the right ingredients and equipment and that it is a recipe you will like.

Before you start on a recipe wash your hands and put on an apron, then collect everything that you will need – it saves a lot of unnecessary walking about. To help you there is a list at the beginning of each recipe.

Measure ingredients carefully and always follow the instructions given. Try to use a standard measuring jug and a set of measuring spoons. When liquids are measured in a measuring jug, check the amount at eye level. For dry ingredients, remember that a level spoon should be levelled off with a knife, a rounded spoon should have as much above as in the bowl of the spoon and for a heaped spoon you take as much as the spoon will hold.

For sticky ingredients like, honey, treacle and syrup, heat the spoon in hot water first and you will find the measured amount slides off easily. For colourings, it's always a good idea to measure the drops into a teaspoon before adding it to the recipe – then if by accident you overdo it, the recipe is not spoilt.

There are lots of recipes where you will have to separate an egg and there is an easy way of doing this. Crack the egg onto a plate, then place a tumbler over the yolk and tip the plate so that the white runs into the mixing basin. Do this carefully because if you want to whisk the egg white there must be no trace of egg yolk or it will not beat up properly.

When you have put things to bake do not open the oven door until the cooking time, indicated in the recipe, has passed — a sudden draught of cold air can make cakes and puddings sink. Always remember to remove baking trays and hot things from the oven using oven gloves.

There are one or two recipes that use a boiling syrup of sugar and water — these should be made with an adult around. A boiling syrup of sugar and water is very hot and should be handled carefully.

Do wash up as you go along, there are usually moments while a recipe is cooking or baking when you can get on with it and then you won't get left with a tiresome pile of dirty dishes at the end.

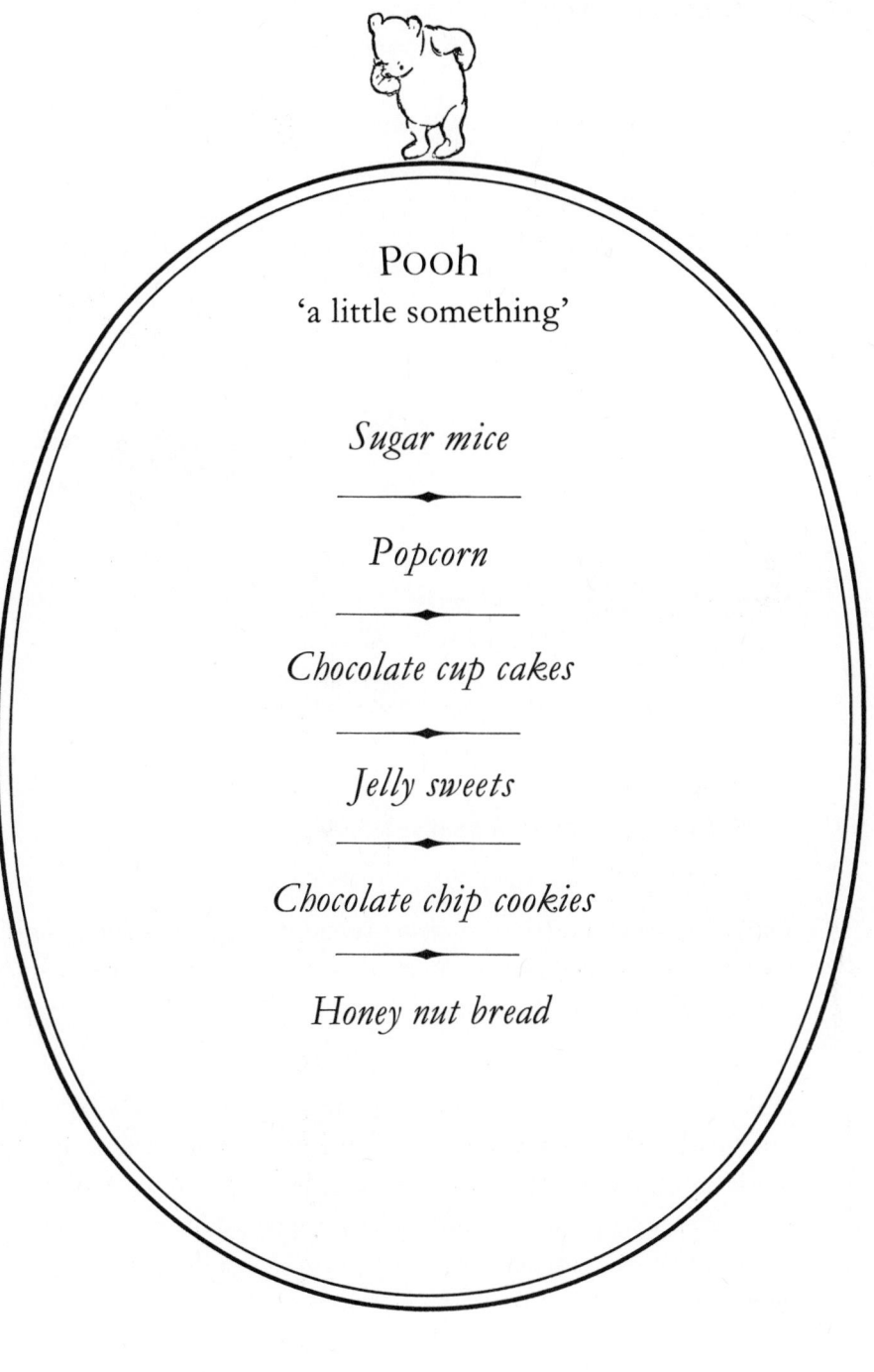

Pooh
'a little something'

Sugar mice

———◆———

Popcorn

———◆———

Chocolate cup cakes

———◆———

Jelly sweets

———◆———

Chocolate chip cookies

———◆———

Honey nut bread

Sugar Mice

Makes 12

12 oz (or 12 heaped tablespoons) icing sugar

1 egg white

1 teaspoon lemon juice

few drops pink or green food colouring

24 silver balls

Find a large mixing basin, a sieve, some greaseproof paper, a fork, a wooden spoon and a knife. You will also need a tray, covered with a sheet of the greaseproof paper, on which to set the mice to dry out.

Sift the icing sugar on to a large sheet of greaseproof paper and put the egg white into the large mixing basin. Using a fork lightly whisk the egg white until frothy. Gradually beat in about two thirds of the sifted icing sugar with a wooden spoon. Add the lemon juice. For green or pink mice, add a few drops of food colouring at this stage.

'I've got a sort of idea,' said Pooh at last, 'but I don't suppose it's a very good one.' 'I don't suppose it is either,' said Eeyore.

Turn the mixture on to a clean working surface and knead in the remaining sugar to get a fondant that is pliable so that you can shape it. Dust the working surface with a little extra icing sugar to prevent the mixture sticking. Shape the fondant into a thick rope and divide into 14 equal pieces.

Reserve two pieces of fondant and shape the remaining 12 into a round, and then elongate each one to make a pear shape with a pointed nose and plump behind. Use the reserved pieces of fondant to provide each mouse with two ears and a tail. Press two silver balls into each one for the eyes.

As you shape each mouse set it on the paper-lined tray. When all are complete put somewhere warm to dry out – an airing cupboard is ideal. These are fun if you use them to decorate a party table.

Popcorn

Serves 3–4

1 tablespoon oil

2 tablespoons popping corn

For popcorn you must have a large saucepan with a tightly fitting lid, and a bowl for serving.

Heat the oil in the saucepan. Add the popcorn and cover the pan with the lid. Wait for the first 'pop' and then shake the pan occasionally, keeping it over the heat until all the corn has popped.

Sweet popcorn – Add 2 tablespoons granulated sugar to the popped corn and shake the pan well. The sugar will melt in the heat of the pan and glaze the popcorn. Turn out into a bowl. The popcorn is very hot at this stage, so don't eat any yet; but as it cools the popcorn will become crisp and crunchy. Then it can be eaten.

Once upon a time, a very long time ago now, about last Friday, Winnie-the-Pooh lived in a forest all by himself under the name of Sanders.

Savoury popcorn – Tip the popped corn out of the saucepan into a bowl. Then sprinkle with salt, or seasoned salt of a flavour you like. Pour over about 1 oz melted butter, toss, and it's ready to eat. If you like you can also sprinkle popcorn with a little grated cheese.

The first thing Pooh did
was to go to the cupboard
to see if he had quite a small
jar of honey left; and he
had, so he took it down.

Chocolate Cup Cakes

Makes 18

4 oz (or 4 rounded tablespoons) self raising flour

1 level teaspoon baking powder

4 oz (or 4 rounded tablespoons) castor sugar

4 oz quick-creaming margarine

2 eggs

1 heaped tablespoon cocoa powder

2 tablespoons boiling water

For the icing:

2 oz (or 2 heaped tablespoons) icing sugar

½ oz (or 1 rounded tablespoon) cocoa powder

1 oz butter

1 oz (or 1 rounded tablespoon) castor sugar

1 tablespoon water

Find a large and a small mixing basin, a sieve, a wooden spoon, a dessertspoon and, for the icing, a small saucepan, a small basin and a teaspoon. You will also need two baking trays and 18 paper baking cases. Arrange the paper cases on the trays. Take the margarine and the eggs out of the refrigerator in advance because this cake is made by an easy, quick mix method and all ingredients must be at room temperature. Turn on the oven heat to moderate (350 °F, 180 °C or Gas No 4), find a pair of oven gloves and a wire cooling tray. Switch on the filled kettle for the hot water.

Sift the flour and the baking powder into the large mixing basin. Add the sugar, the margarine and the eggs. Measure the cocoa powder into the small basin, add the hot water and mix to a paste. Add the cocoa paste to the ingredients in the large basin. Using a wooden spoon, stir first to blend the ingredients, then beat hard for 1 minute to make a smooth cake batter.

Carefully put about half a dessertspoon of cake mixture into each paper baking case. Place in the pre-heated oven and bake for 20–25 minutes or until well risen and springy to the touch. Let the cakes cool on a wire cooling tray.

Meanwhile prepare the icing. Sift the icing sugar and cocoa powder into the small basin. Measure the butter, sugar and water into the saucepan. Stir over low heat to melt the butter and bring just to the boil. Then pour all at once into the sifted ingredients and using a wooden spoon beat to a smooth, soft chocolate icing.

Let the icing cool until it becomes thick enough to spread. Then put a teaspoonful on each little cake and spread flat. Leave until the icing has set firm.

Jelly Sweets

Makes 36

4 tablespoons water

2 level tablespoons powdered gelatine

1 lb granulated sugar

generous ¼ pint (or 6 fl oz) water

1 teaspoon fruit flavouring – raspberry, lemon or orange

½ level teaspoon citric acid dissolved in 1 tablespoon water

few drops of food colouring to suit the flavour chosen

castor sugar to coat the finished jellies

Find a medium-sized saucepan, a wooden spoon and a sugar boiling thermometer (optional – see below). Get out a small mixing basin and a clean pastry brush. You will also need a 7″ (18 cm) shallow square tin for the jelly sweets to set in. Grease the pan well with butter. Food colourings and essences are easy to find in a supermarket and the citric acid is usually sold in a chemist's shop. When the jelly sweets are ready to turn out, you will need a knife for cutting them up.

Measure the 4 tablespoons of water into one small basin and sprinkle in the gelatine powder. Set aside to soak for at least 5 minutes.

Measure the granulated sugar and the generous ¼ pint water into the saucepan. Using a wooden spoon, stir gently over a low heat until the sugar has dissolved. Make sure there are no sugar crystals by brushing down the inside of the pan with a pastry brush dipped in a little cold water.

'A party for Me?'
thought Pooh to himself.
'How grand!'

Fix the sugar thermometer to the inside of the pan (they usually have a clip on the back) so that the base is in the syrup and bring to the boil. Boil without stirring until the temperature on the thermometer reads 240 °F (120 °C) or, if you have no thermometer, until a little of the syrup dropped from a teaspoon into a saucer of cold water forms a soft ball when picked up in the fingers.

Draw off the heat and add the cake of soaked gelatine. Stir until the gelatine has dissolved. Then add the flavouring of your choice, the dissolved citric acid and a few drops of colouring. Pour into the greased pan and leave for several hours or overnight until set.

To turn out, sprinkle a little castor sugar over the top, then take hold of the mixture at one corner and pull out of the tin. Turn on to a bed of castor sugar. Using a sharp knife cut first into strips and then into squares, dipping the cut edges into the sugar each time so that they don't stick.

You can make a pretty table decoration that can be eaten by piercing jelly sweets with a cocktail stick and spiking them into whole grapefruits like a 'porcupine'. Set the fruit in sundae glasses to get height and to hold it steady.

'What about a mouthful of something?' Pooh always liked a
little something at eleven o'clock in the morning.

Chocolate Chip Cookies

Makes 36
5 oz (or 5 rounded tablespoons) plain flour
¼ level teaspoon bicarbonate of soda
¼ level teaspoon salt
4 oz butter
2 oz (or 2 rounded tablespoons) soft brown sugar
3 oz (or 3 rounded tablespoons) castor sugar
1 egg
few drops vanilla essence
1 (4 oz) packet chocolate chips
1 oz (or 1 heaped tablespoon) finely chopped walnuts

Find a large and a small mixing basin, a large plate, a sieve, a
wooden spoon, a fork and a teaspoon for shaping the cookies. You
will also need two baking trays which should be well greased. Turn
the oven heat to moderately hot (375 °F, 190 °C or Gas No 5), find
a pair of oven gloves, a wire cooling tray and a palette knife with
which to lift off the baked cookies.

Sift the flour, bicarbonate of soda and the salt on to a large plate and set aside. Put the butter and both sugars in the large basin and using a wooden spoon beat until soft and light.

In the small basin lightly mix the egg and vanilla essence with a fork. Gradually beat the mixed egg into the creamed mixture. Stir in the sifted flour and beat until smooth. Then mix in the chocolate chips and the chopped walnuts.

Spoon teaspoonfuls of the mixture on to the greased baking trays. Space the cookies a little apart to allow room for spreading. You will get about 12 cookies on a tray so this recipe will have to be baked in batches.

Place the cookies in the pre-heated oven and bake for 12 minutes or until golden brown. Using a palette knife transfer the baked cookies from the tray on to a wire cooling tray. They will become crisp as they cool.

Honey Nut Bread

Makes 1 large loaf

12 oz (or 12 rounded tablespoons) self raising flour

pinch of salt

3 oz (or 3 rounded tablespoons) soft brown sugar

2 oz (or 3 rounded tablespoons) chopped walnuts

2 eggs

3 tablespoons clear honey

scant ½ pint (9 fl oz) milk

2 oz butter

You will need 2 mixing basins, a sieve, a whisk and a wooden spoon for mixing the bread and a small saucepan for melting the butter. Find a large 9″×5″×2″ (23 cm×13 cm×5 cm) loaf pan, grease it well and line the base with a strip of greased greaseproof paper. Turn the oven heat to moderate (350 °F, 180 °C or Gas No 4), find a pair of oven gloves and a wire cooling tray.

'Well, good-bye, if you're sure you won't have any more.'
'**Is** there any more?' asked Pooh quickly.

Sift the flour and the salt into the large mixing basin. Add the sugar and the chopped walnuts and mix thoroughly. Make a well in the centre of the ingredients.

Put the eggs into the second mixing basin, add the honey and the milk. Whisk well to mix them thoroughly. Melt the butter in a saucepan over low heat.

Add the egg, honey and milk mixture to the dry ingredients and, using a wooden spoon, stir first to blend and then beat well to get a smooth batter. Add the melted butter and stir thoroughly.

Turn the mixture into the prepared loaf pan and spread level. Place in the centre of the pre-heated oven and bake for 1 hour. Remove from the tin and while hot rub over with a buttered paper to make it shiny. Allow to cool. Then serve sliced, spread with butter. This bread makes tasty sandwiches with cream cheese.

Owl
teatime and party ideas

Party dip

Cheese straws and biscuits

Sandwich kebabs

Hot bacon savouries

Butterfly cakes

Orange jellies

Chocolate mousse

Party Dip

Serves 8–12

8 oz full fat soft cream cheese

3 tablespoons prepared oil and vinegar dressing (see page 64 for this)

2 tablespoons tomato ketchup

2 teaspoons finely chopped or grated onion

crisp vegetables or salty biscuits for dipping

You will need a wooden spoon and a mixing basin, a chopping board and a knife. For serving the dip, place a small bowl in the centre of a round tray or large plate. Then you can surround the dip with selected items for dipping.

Put the cream cheese in the mixing basin and using a wooden spoon beat until soft and smooth. Add the oil and vinegar dressing, tomato ketchup and chopped onion, and mix well to get a soft dipping consistency. Spoon into the serving bowl.

Choose fresh vegetables in season – peeled and sliced carrot sticks, or cucumber or fresh radishes. Wash well and when prepared store in a polythene bag in the refrigerator to crisp. Carrot sticks are best dropped in iced water for an hour before the party. You can also include some salty biscuits or crackers. Group these items attractively around the dip for serving.

'Owl,' said Christopher Robin, 'I am going to give a party.'

Cheese Straws and Biscuits

Makes 48 cheese straws or 24 cheese biscuits

4 oz (or 4 rounded tablespoons) self raising flour

½ level teaspoon salt

pinch dry mustard

1½ oz butter

1 oz white cooking fat

2 oz (or 2 heaped tablespoons) grated cheddar cheese

2 tablespoons cold water to mix

Find a large mixing basin, a sieve, a fork for mixing, a pastry board and a rolling pin. You will need a plate for blending the fat, a table knife for mixing and a sharp knife for cutting. If you make cheese biscuits you will need a 2″ (5 cm) round biscuit cutter. You will also require 2 baking trays which should be well greased. Turn the oven heat to moderate (350 °F, 180 °C or Gas No 4) and find a pair of oven gloves and a wire cooling tray.

Sift the flour, salt and mustard powder into the large mixing basin. Measure the butter and cooking fat on to a plate and beat them together with a table knife. Add to the flour and using finger tips rub into the mixture. Add the grated cheese and mix thoroughly. Then sprinkle in the water and using a fork mix to a rough dough in the basin.

Turn the dough out on to a floured pastry board and knead lightly to get a smooth pastry. Roll out the pastry to a thickness of about ¼″ (6 mm).

He could spell his own
name WOL.

Cheese straws – Cut the rolled out pastry into strips of about 3″
(7·5 cm) wide, using a sharp knife. Then cut across into strips of
about ½″ (1 cm) wide. Pick each strip up and transfer to a baking
tray, twisting it (like barley sugar) as you set it down. Arrange
neatly so that you can get them all on the trays.

Cheese biscuits – Prick the pastry all over with a fork. Then using
a floured cutter, stamp out circles of the pastry. Transfer these
carefully to the baking trays.

Place straws or biscuits in the centre of the pre-heated oven and
bake for 10–12 minutes or until golden brown and crisp – biscuits
will take longer than straws. Let cool on a wire cooling tray. The
cheese straws look pretty piled in a dish. The biscuits can be eaten
as they are or you can spread them with herb cheese, liver pâté or
other savoury toppings for a party.

'What did you do?'
'Nothing.'
'The best thing,' said Owl
wisely.

Sandwich Kebabs

Makes 12

4 slices of white bread from a sandwich loaf
4 slices of brown bread from a large loaf
butter for spreading
Marmite
2–4 crisp lettuce leaves
1 oz liver pâté
mustard and cress for serving

You will need a chopping board on which to work, a table knife for spreading and a kitchen knife for cutting. Find two squares of kitchen foil for wrapping the sandwiches and 12 wooden cocktail sticks for serving. Select a serving plate and cover it with a paper doily.

Lettuce and Marmite – Spread four slices of white bread with butter and add a light coating of Marmite to two of them. Top these two with crisp lettuce and cover with the remaining two bread slices buttered side down. Press gently together.

Liver pâté – Spread four slices of brown bread with butter and then spread two of them with liver pâté. Top with the remaining bread slices, buttered side down. Press gently together.

Wrap the sandwiches in foil and put in the refrigerator for 2 hours. To serve unwrap and cut away all the crusts with a knife. Then cut each sandwich lengthwise and crosswise three times to make 9 small squares or 'mini' sandwiches. Spike these mini sandwiches – two white and one brown or *vice versa* on to cocktail sticks. Arrange on a plate and sprinkle with mustard and cress. Allow two or three sandwich kebabs per person.

Hot Bacon Savouries

Makes 24

12 rashers streaky bacon

1 (12 oz) tin pineapple cubes

Find a chopping board, a knife and kitchen scissors to trim the rashers. You will also need 3–4 long kebab skewers on which to spear the savouries for grilling, a fork, oven gloves and 24 wooden cocktail sticks for serving. You can get these ready in advance and then grill the savouries when required.

Trim the rinds from the bacon rashers with the kitchen scissors and drain the pineapple cubes from the juice in the tin. Stretch the bacon rashers in turn by pressing them flat along the chopping board with the blade of a knife. Cut each rasher in half. Then wrap one bacon piece round each pineapple cube.

As they are prepared, thread the bacon savouries close together on long skewers ready for grilling. Just before serving, place the skewers together under a pre-heated hot grill. Let them cook for 3–4 minutes, turning the skewers over so that the savouries cook both sides – the bacon will crisp up well.

When ready push the savouries off the skewers, using a fork, and spike each one with a cocktail stick. Arrange on a plate and serve hot.

Kanga was down below tying the things on, and calling out to Owl, 'You won't want this dirty old dish-cloth any more, will you, and what about this carpet, it's all in holes,' and Owl was calling back indignantly, 'Of course I do! It's just a question of arranging the furniture properly, and it isn't a dish-cloth, it's my shawl.

Butterfly Cakes

Makes 12

4 oz (or 4 rounded tablespoons) self raising flour

pinch salt

3 oz butter

3 oz (or 3 rounded tablespoons) castor sugar

1 egg

few drops vanilla essence

1–2 tablespoons milk to mix

For the buttercream icing:

2 oz butter

3 oz (or 3 heaped tablespoons) icing sugar

few drops vanilla essence

extra icing sugar for dusting

You will need a large and a small mixing basin, a sieve, a large plate, a wooden spoon, a tablespoon, a teaspoon and a small vegetable knife for cutting out the tops of the cakes. Find one baking tray and set on it 12 paper baking cases. Turn the oven heat to moderately hot (375 °F, 190 °C or Gas No 5) and find a pair of oven gloves and a wire cooling tray.

Sift the flour and salt on to a plate and set aside. Put the butter and sugar into the large basin and beat with a wooden spoon until soft and creamy.

Oh, the butterflies are flying,
Now the winter days are dying,
And the primroses are trying
    To be seen.

Lightly mix the egg and vanilla essence with a fork in the small basin. Then gradually beat into the creamed mixture a little at a time. Beat well, adding a little of the sifted flour along with the last few additions of egg. Then using a metal spoon fold in the remaining flour and just sufficient milk to make a soft dropping consistency.

Place half a dessertspoon of the cake mixture in each of the paper baking cases. Place the cakes in the pre-heated oven and bake for 20–25 minutes or until they are risen and brown. Wearing oven gloves, take the cakes from the oven and let them cool on a wire cooling tray.

Meanwhile cream the butter for the buttercream icing until soft. Gradually beat in the sifted icing sugar and mix until smooth. Flavour with a few drops of vanilla essence.

When the cakes are cold, cut a slice from the top of each one, holding the knife so that it slopes slightly inwards. You will cut away what looks like a shallow round 'cone' of cake. Cut each piece in half and set beside the cake from which it has been cut.

Place a teaspoon of buttercream in the centre of each cake, and replace the two semi-circular pieces, pressing them into the buttercream so that they stand up like the wings of a butterfly. Dust the cakes with icing sugar and they are ready to serve.

Orange Jellies

Serves 8
4 medium sized oranges
1 strawberry jelly
water – see recipe

Find a chopping board and a kitchen knife, a small basin, a lemon squeezer, a teaspoon, kitchen scissors and a measuring jug in which to make up the jelly. You will also need a dish in which to balance the orange halves while they set or, preferably, a tray of patty tins in which to hold them steady. Fill and switch on the kettle for boiling water.

Cut the oranges in half and squeeze out the juice. Handle the oranges carefully so that the shells are not broken. You can pass the orange juice around for drinking as it is not required in this recipe.

Pull the pith and pulp from the inside of each orange half. Do this by pushing the finger tips, or the handle of a teaspoon, down between the pith and the outer orange peel so that you can get hold of it, then pull and the pith and pulp should come out quite easily. Take care not to make a hole in the base and if necessary snip the last bit of the pith out with kitchen scissors. Set the oranges in a dish or a tray of patty tins to hold them steady.

Separate the squares of strawberry jelly and put them in a measuring jug; make up to ½ pint with boiling water. Stir until the jelly has dissolved. Then make up to just under a pint (18 fl oz) with cold water or ice cubes – stir the ice cubes until dissolved.

'Well,' said Owl, 'the customary procedure in such cases is as follows.'

'What does Crustimoney Proceedcake mean?' said Pooh. 'For I am a Bear of Very Little Brain, and long words Bother me.'

Let the jelly stand until quite cold and showing signs of setting – give a stir once or twice to check. Then pour the almost setting jelly into each orange half and fill to the brim. Chill the orange jellies in the refrigerator until firm.

Cut each orange jelly in half to make quarters and arrange on a serving dish. These look pretty set around a bowl filled with scoops of vanilla ice cream for serving.

Chocolate Mousse

Serves 4

4 oz plain chocolate

½ oz butter

4 eggs

Find a large saucepan and a mixing basin, that will fit snugly over it for melting the chocolate. A second basin will be required for whisking the egg whites and you will need a whisk, a wooden spoon and a tablespoon. Set out four individual serving glasses for the finished mousse. Half fill the saucepan with hot water and set the mixing basin over the top.

Oh, the honey-bees are gumming
On their little wings, and humming
That the summer, which is coming,
    Will be fun.

Break the chocolate into the basin. Stir occasionally until the chocolate has melted, then add the butter and stir well to mix.

Separate the eggs, putting the whites into the second basin. Add the yolks to the chocolate mixture. Stir the yolks and chocolate together thoroughly and then remove the bowl from the heat.

Whisk the egg whites until stiff. Then using a metal spoon fold them gently but evenly into the chocolate mixture. Pour the chocolate mousse into the serving glasses. Chill in the refrigerator until the mousse is quite firm – about 2–3 hours.

This chocolate mousse is very attractive decorated with pieces of tinned pineapple – the sharp flavour of the pineapple counteracts the richness of the chocolate mixture.

Piglet
snack and supper things

Risotto

———————◆———————

Eggs baked in the oven

———————◆———————

Beefburgers

———————◆———————

Kedgeree

———————◆———————

Curried eggs and rice

———————◆———————

Fried ham sandwiches

'I'm planting a haycorn, Pooh, so that it can grow up into an oak-tree, and have lots of haycorns just outside the front door instead of having to walk miles and miles, do you see, Pooh?'

Risotto

Serves 4

8 oz (or 8 rounded tablespoons) long grain rice

4 rashers lean bacon

1 small onion

1 pint hot stock (made using 1 chicken cube and water)

1½ oz butter

salt and freshly milled pepper

4 oz button mushrooms

2 oz (or 2 heaped tablespoons) grated cheddar cheese

You will need a medium sized saucepan with a lid to fit, a small frying pan, a chopping board, a kitchen knife, kitchen scissors, a wooden spoon and a measuring jug for making up the stock. Find a pretty serving dish for the risotto and put it to warm. Switch on the filled kettle for boiling water.

Pick over the rice, removing any dark grains, but do not wash or rinse because wet rice will stick to the pan when you fry it. Trim the rinds from the bacon rashers with the scissors and then cut the bacon into pieces. Peel and chop the onion fairly small.

Melt 1 oz of the butter in the saucepan, add the bacon pieces and the chopped onion and let them fry gently for a few minutes to soften the onion and draw the fat from the bacon. Then add the rice and stir to mix. Season with salt and pepper and gently stir in the hot stock. Stir until the mixture is boiling, then lower the heat to a simmer and cover the pan with the lid. Let the risotto simmer gently for 20–30 minutes or until the rice is tender and all the liquid is absorbed.

Meanwhile wipe the mushrooms clean and then slice them thinly. Melt the remaining butter in the small frying pan, add the mushrooms and turn them gently in the hot butter for 3–4 minutes only.

When the rice is cooked, gently fold in the mushrooms and half the grated cheese with a fork. Turn the risotto into the hot serving dish, sprinkle with the remaining grated cheese and serve.

'Pooh!' squeaked the voice.
'It's Piglet!' cried Pooh eagerly. 'Where are you?'
'Underneath,' said Piglet in an underneath sort of way.
'Underneath what?'
'You,' squeaked Piglet. 'Get up!'

Eggs Baked in the Oven

Serves 4

4 eggs

salt and freshly milled pepper

4 tablespoons single cream

For these you will need 'ramekin' dishes, which are little individual baking dishes, and a tablespoon for measuring the cream. Turn the oven heat to moderate (350 °F, 180 °C or Gas No 4) and put in the ramekin dishes to warm. Then butter the dishes well and set them in a roasting tin. Fill and switch on the kettle for boiling water and find a pair of oven gloves.

Crack one egg into each ramekin dish. Season each egg with salt and pepper. Pour sufficient hot water into the roasting tin to come half way up the sides of the dishes.

Put the eggs in the centre of the pre-heated oven and let them cook for about 6 minutes or until the egg whites are barely set.

Carefully take the eggs from the oven (wearing oven gloves, of course) and pour 1 tablespoon of cream on each one. Replace them in the oven and let cook for about 4–5 minutes more. When ready the egg whites will be set, but the yolks still runny.

These are very good served with hot toast. If you like you can sprinkle a little chopped parsley or grated cheese on the eggs after adding the cream and before putting them back in the oven.

Then Piglet (PIGLET) thought a thing:
  'Courage!' he said. 'There's always hope.
I want a thinnish piece of rope.
Or, if there isn't any, bring
A thickish piece of string.'

Beefburgers

Serves 4

1 slice white bread

1–2 tablespoons milk

12 oz lean minced beef

1 onion

½ level teaspoon salt

freshly milled pepper

1 egg

seasoned flour*

1 oz butter for frying

4 soft rolls

You will need a chopping board, a kitchen knife, a medium sized mixing basin, a wooden spoon, a fork, a good sized frying pan and a fish slice for turning the burgers while they are cooking and for serving. Cut the soft rolls in half and have them ready for toasting under the grill. It is also a good idea to have a few onion slices and some mustard or tomato ketchup for serving.

Trim the crusts from the slice of bread and crumble the white part into the mixing basin. Add just enough milk to soak up the bread, then mix with a fork to break it up. Add the minced beef, the peeled and finely chopped onion, the salt, a seasoning of pepper and the egg. Mix very well with the fork until the ingredients bind together.

Divide the mixture into four equal portions. With wetted fingers shape each portion into a round and then flatten them slightly. Roll each one in seasoned flour.

Melt the butter in the frying pan and when hot add the 'burgers'. Fry fairly quickly to brown both sides. Then lower the heat, cover the pan with a lid and cook them gently for 25–30 minutes. Turn them once during frying so that they cook evenly.

When cooked lift out carefully and slide each one into a toasted split roll. Serve with a slice or two of onion or a little mustard or ketchup in each one. Wrap in a paper napkin and eat in the fingers.

* Seasoned flour is just plain flour with a little salt and pepper added for flavour

Kedgeree

Serves 4

1 medium sized smoked haddock on the bone

few stalks of fresh parsley

8 oz (or 8 rounded tablespoons) long grain rice

1 small onion

1½ oz butter

pinch curry powder

freshly milled pepper

1 pint hot fish stock – see below

squeeze of lemon juice

1 egg

You will need a chopping board, a kitchen knife, a fork, a medium sized saucepan with a lid that fits and a measuring jug for the stock. Find a serving dish for the kedgeree and put it to warm. Hard boil the egg for 8 minutes in boiling water.

Rinse and cut up the haddock so that you can put the pieces in the saucepan. Add water to cover – about a generous 1 pint. Nip the curly leaves off the parsley and reserve for later. Put the parsley stalks in with the fish.

Set the pan over the heat and bring to the boil. Then lower the heat to a simmer, cover the pan with a lid and cook very gently for about 10 minutes or until the fish is cooked. Draw off the heat and strain the cooking liquid into a measuring jug. This is your fish stock. Check that the amount is 1 pint – if not make it up with water. Set the cooked fish aside to cool and rinse out the saucepan.

The wind was against them now, and Piglet's ears

streamed behind him

like banners

Pick over the rice and remove any dark grains. Peel and finely chop the onion. Melt 1 oz of the butter in the saucepan, add the chopped onion and cook gently for a few minutes to soften. Add a pinch of curry powder and let cook for a moment longer – curry adds a spicy flavour to kedgeree. Stir in the rice.

Gradually add the hot fish stock. Stir until boiling, then lower the heat to a simmer, cover the pan with a lid and cook very gently for 20–30 minutes or until the rice is tender and all the liquid absorbed.

Meanwhile remove the skin and any bones from the cooked haddock. Break the flesh into flakes. When the rice is ready fold in the flaked fish with a fork. Add a good seasoning of freshly milled pepper, a squeeze of lemon juice and the rest of the butter in flakes.

Pile the kedgeree into the hot serving dish. Garnish with the hard boiled egg cut in quarters and the reserved parsley tops which have been very finely chopped.

Curried Eggs and Rice

Serves 4

4 eggs

6 oz (or 6 rounded tablespoons) long grain rice

For the curry sauce:

1 oz butter

1 onion

½ cooking apple

2 level tablespoons curry powder

1 level tablespoon flour

½ pint chicken stock (made using ½ a chicken cube and water)

1 dessertspoon mango chutney or apricot jam

1 oz (or 1 rounded tablespoon) brown sugar

juice of ½ lemon

1 tablespoon sultanas

You will need a chopping board, a vegetable peeler and a vegetable knife; two saucepans, a colander or sieve for straining the rice, a roasting tin in which to keep it hot and a piece of kitchen foil for covering the tin. You will also need a bowl in which to keep the eggs and a wooden spoon for stirring the sauce. Choose a dish for serving the rice and one for the curried eggs. Turn the oven heat to slow (250 °F, 130 °C or Gas No ½) and put the dishes to warm. Find a pair of oven gloves.

'Perhaps he won't notice **you,** Piglet,' said Pooh
encouragingly, 'because you're a Very Small Animal.'

Hard boil the eggs for 8 minutes in boiling water. Cool them
quickly under running cold water, remove the shells and keep the
eggs submerged in a bowl of cold water while making the sauce.

Peel and chop the onion and peel and dice the apple. Melt the
butter in the saucepan over low heat and add the onion. Cook gently
for 3–4 minutes or until the onion has softened, then add the apple
and the curry powder. Stir over the heat for a moment to draw the
flavour from the curry powder and then stir in the flour.

Gradually stir in the stock and bring the sauce to the boil. Add
the chutney (chop up any large pieces) or apricot jam, the sugar,
lemon juice and sultanas. Cover the pan with a lid and simmer
gently for about 30 minutes.

Meanwhile bring a pan of salted water to the boil for the rice.
Add the rice to the water and stir with a wooden spoon until the
water reboils. Then cook the rice for 8–10 minutes or until tender.
Test the rice by scooping out a grain and pressing it gently between
the fingers – there should be no hard core. Drain the rice in a
colander. Then rinse the rice (in the colander) under hot water and
spread it out in a roasting tin. Cover the tin with a piece of kitchen
foil. But in the oven to keep warm until you are ready to serve it.

When the sauce is ready, slice the hard boiled eggs in half and
arrange in the serving dish. Pour the curry sauce over the eggs.
Then stir up the rice with a fork and serve.

In a corner of the room, the table-cloth began to

wriggle.

Fried Ham Sandwiches

Serves 2

4 slices of white bread
butter for spreading
2 slices of ham
little prepared mustard
1 egg
1 tablespoon milk
1 oz butter for frying

Find a cutting board, a kitchen knife, a fork and a table knife for spreading the butter. You will also need a shallow dish or soup plate for dipping the sandwiches and a frying pan for cooking them. A fish slice is useful for turning the sandwiches over and for lifting them out of the pan. Since these must be eaten hot and newly cooked, put two serving plates to warm and have knives and forks ready.

Then it jumped up
and
down once or twice, and put out two ears. It rolled across
the room again, and unwound itself.

Spread the slices of bread with butter on one side only. Top two
of the slices with a slice of ham and just a smear of mustard. Cover
with remaining bread slices, buttered side down, and press gently.
Trim away the crusts and cut each sandwich in half.

Crack the egg into the shallow dish, add the milk and a seasoning
of salt and pepper. Whisk with a fork to mix.

Melt the butter in a frying pan. Dip the bread sandwiches both
sides in the egg and milk mixture. Allow egg mixture to soak in for
a moment, then lift out allowing any excess to drain off. Add the
sandwiches to the hot melted butter. Fry over moderate heat until
brown on both sides – turn them over fairly frequently so that they
cook evenly. Then lift from the pan and serve at once. These are
nice with grilled tomatoes.

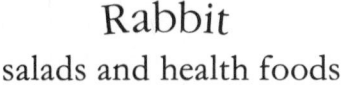

Rabbit
salads and health foods

Apple coleslaw

———◆———

Muesli

———◆———

Home-made yogurt

———◆———

Herb cheese

———◆———

Tomato and spring onion salad

———◆———

Bread and butter pickles

———◆———

Herb bread

'It all comes,' said Pooh crossly,
'of not having front doors big enough.'
'It all comes,' said Rabbit sternly,
'of eating too much.'

Apple Coleslaw

Serves 6

¼–½ head of white or summer cabbage – see below

2 dessert apples

2 tablespoons seedless raisins

3 tablespoons prepared oil and vinegar dressing (see page 64 for recipe)

2 rounded tablespoons mayonnaise

1 tablespoon salted peanuts

Find a chopping board and a sharp kitchen knife. You will need a clean tea towel to dry the shredded cabbage, a small vegetable knife, a tablespoon, a good sized mixing basin in which to prepare the salad and a china or wooden bowl for serving it.

Cabbage shreds up into a lot of salad – from a tightly packed head you will only need about a quarter to make enough for six servings. Summer cabbages are often more open and in this case you will need about half the head. Remove any outer damaged or coarse leaves. Cut the cabbage half through again to make two quarters. Slice away any core.

With one hand press the cut side of the cabbage firmly downwards on a chopping board and slice the leaves into fine shreds. Wash the cabbage shreds in cold salted water and then drain in a colander. Pat or shake dry in a clean tea towel and put the cabbage in a mixing basin.

Peel, core and cut the apple up into chunky pieces and add to the cabbage along with the seedless raisins and the oil and vinegar dressing. Toss ingredients to mix.

Cover the bowl with a piece of transparent film wrap or a plate and put to chill in the refrigerator for at least 30 minutes.

Add the mayonnaise and salted peanuts and toss again to mix. Turn the salad into the serving bowl. This goes well with cold meats and in particular with sliced ham.

Muesli

Serves 3

2 oz (or 4 heaped tablespoons) rolled oats
1 oz (or 1 rounded tablespoon) soft brown sugar
2 tablespoons wheat germ
2 tablespoons bran
2 tablespoons seedless raisins
1 tablespoon chopped roasted hazelnuts

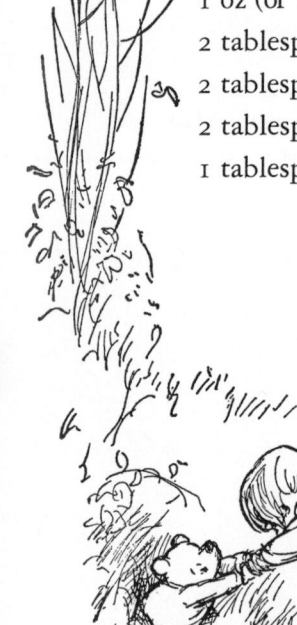

You only need a bowl and a measuring spoon for this. If you want to make up and keep your own muesli you will need a container with a tight fitting lid to keep it fresh. Serve muesli for breakfast in place of ordinary cereal.

Measure all the ingredients into the bowl and mix well. To use – measure out 3 tablespoons of the mixture into each serving bowl.

Top with grated dessert apple, sliced banana or any stewed fruit that you like. Eat with milk or natural yogurt.

Home-Made Yogurt

Serves 6

2 pints UHT milk – see below

1 carton plain yogurt

This recipe shows you how to make yogurt with the things you have in the kitchen. Find a serving bowl that has a capacity of 2½ pints into which you will put the yogurt to set, a plate to fit over the top and a few clean tea towels to wrap around and over the yogurt to keep it warm while setting – they won't get dirty. You will also need a large saucepan, a fork, a whisk and a sugar-boiling thermometer which is not essential but does help you to check the temperature accurately.

For this method it is important to use ultra heat treated (UHT) or 'Long Life' milk which comes in cartons – make sure you get the right one. If the yogurt you have bought for the starter is in the refrigerator, take it out so that it is at room temperature for using. Put the serving bowl and the plate to warm before you start.

Pour the milk into the saucepan and heat gently until it is slightly hotter than lukewarm – a few drops on the wrist should feel hot, but not burning and you should be able to hold your hand comfortably against the side of the pan. If possible use a sugar-boiling thermometer to check the temperature which should read 110 °F (43 °C). Draw the pan off the heat.

'Now,' said Rabbit, 'this is a Search, and I've Organized it.'

Stir the carton of yogurt with a fork until creamy and add to the milk. Whisk well to combine the two and make the milk frothy. Pour into the warm serving bowl and place the warmed plate over the top. Set the bowl of yogurt in a warm place with towels under, around and over the top to insulate the heat and hold the temperature of the milk.

Leave undisturbed for at least 6 hours, after which time you can have a peep. Shake the dish gently and if the yogurt has set, take it out and put immediately in the refrigerator. Chill well before eating. The yogurt will keep for up to 2 days in the refrigerator.

Spoon the yogurt straight from the bowl and sprinkle with brown sugar or castor sugar when it will taste delicious. Or you can make fruit flavours by stirring in puréed fruits like strawberries or raspberries, a little Ribena or concentrated orange juice.

'If I know anything about anything, that hole means Rabbit,'
he said, 'and Rabbit means Company,' he said, 'and Company
means Food.'

Herb Cheese

Serves 3
1 pint milk
juice of 1 lemon
salt and freshly milled pepper
2 tablespoons single cream
chopped chives or spring onion

Find a medium sized saucepan and a wooden spoon. A sugar boiling
thermometer is not essential but is a help to judge the temperature
of the milk. You will also need a large square of double thickness
butter muslin and a colander for straining the cheese. Later on you
will need a mixing basin, a chopping board, a fork and a kitchen
knife for making up the cheese mixture. Before you start find a
hook, or fix something on from which to hang the cheese to drain.
The bar under a kitchen stool will do, or even a rod across the top
of a bucket. Put a bowl underneath to catch the drips.

Pour the milk into the saucepan and heat gently until slightly
hotter than lukewarm – a few drops on the wrist should feel hot
but not burning and you should be able to hold your hand comfortably against the side of the pan. If possible use a sugar-boiling
thermometer to check the temperature of the milk which should
read 100 °F (38 °C). Draw the pan off the heat.

Stir the lemon juice into the milk and let stand for 15 minutes. You will see the curds separating before your eyes.

Line the colander (set over a dish) with the square of double thickness butter muslin. Pour in the milk mixture. Carefully knot the opposite corners of the muslin and pick the bag up. Hang the cheese to drain and after an hour or so the curds will be dry enough to use.

Tip the curds into the mixing basin. Add salt and pepper to taste and the cream. Whip with a fork to a smooth consistency. Stir in the finely chopped chives or spring onion. In winter time you can add a little chopped onion and parsley.

Any curd cheese like this is a change from butter in sandwiches, and it goes particularly well with ham or cucumber and with watercress. It is also good spread on slices of hot buttered toast, or you can use it to top split and buttered cheese scones for tea.

For the spring is really springing,
You can see a skylark singing,
And the blue-bells, which are ringing,
Can be heard.

Tomato and Spring Onion Salad

Serves 4

1 lb fresh tomatoes

4–6 spring onions

1 tablespoon chopped parsley

For the dressing:

salt and freshly milled pepper

1 teaspoon castor sugar

1 tablespoon wine vinegar

3 tablespoons oil

You will need a large mixing basin in which to scald the tomatoes, a chopping board and a vegetable knife. Find a small basin for the dressing, a tablespoon and a fork. Select a pretty serving bowl for the salad and put the filled kettle on for boiling water.

Nick the skins of the tomatoes and put them all together in a large mixing basin. Pour over boiling water to cover and let the tomatoes stand for about 1 minute. As soon as the skins begin to curl back from the tiny nick, pour off the water. Run the tomatoes under cold water to prevent them from becoming too soft. Carefully peel away the skin from each.

Slice the tomatoes across, and arrange in a salad bowl. Wash, peel and then trim the roots and the top coarse green parts from the spring onions. Then finely shred the white bulb and some of the tender green of the stem of each one. Add the spring onions to the tomatoes.

For the dressing put a seasoning of salt and pepper into a small basin. Add the vinegar and stir with a fork to dissolve the seasonings. Add the oil and whisk with the fork to get an emulsion.

Pour the dressing over the tomatoes and let the salad stand for at least 1 hour so that the dressing draws the juices from the tomatoes and the flavours mingle.

Sprinkle with chopped parsley and serve. This salad is good on its own and is also very tasty with cold meats.

Bread and Butter Pickles

Makes 1 large jar

3 large cucumbers

2 large onions

2 oz (2 rounded tablespoons) cooking salt

For the syrup:

1 pint white wine vinegar

1 lb soft brown sugar

½ level teaspoon ground turmeric

¼ level teaspoon ground cloves

1 tablespoon whole mustard seed

You will need a large mixing basin, a plate to put on top of the pickles and a good sized saucepan to cook them in. In addition you should get out a chopping board, a kitchen knife, a colander and a perforated spoon. For the finished pickles you will need either a medium sized glass knob-stoppered jar (which looks pretty) or a deep polythene refrigerator box with a fitting lid. Do not leave any of the spices out, particularly the turmeric which gives a lovely colour – you can buy them in a supermarket or a chemist's shop.

These pickles are delicious to eat and you can spread them on bread and butter which is how they got their name. Make them in summer when there are lots of cheap cucumbers, and they will last all the year. Wash the cucumbers, but do not peel and slice them very thinly. Peel and thinly slice the onions.

Arrange layers of onion and cucumber slices and salt in the large mixing basin. Weight them down with a plate and let them stand for about 3 hours. The salt draws the juices from the vegetables and you will soon find that the vegetables are beginning to float in the salty liquid in the basin. Pour this liquid away and rinse the cucumber and onion slices under running cold water. Drain well in the colander.

Put the vinegar, sugar and spices into the saucepan and stir over low heat to dissolve the sugar. Add the cucumber and onion slices and bring to the boil. Cook for 2 minutes only – otherwise you soften the vegetables too much. Draw the pan off the heat.

Using a perforated spoon scoop out the cucumber, onion and the spices and put them into a glass knob-stoppered jar or a suitable container.

Replace the pan of syrup over the heat and let it simmer for about 15 minutes to reduce and concentrate the flavour. Then pour the syrup over the vegetables. If you have judged it well there should be just enough syrup to cover them. Let the pickles cool, then cover and store.

You can eat these as soon as they are made but they do taste even better after a month or so. Try the bread and butter pickles with cold meat, or spike them with cubes of cheese on cocktail sticks for a party.

Herb Bread

Serves 6

2 Vienna loaves
4 oz butter
1 tablespoon lemon juice
1 tablespoon chopped parsley
1 tablespoon chopped chives

You will need a bread board and a knife for cutting the loaves, and two large squares of kitchen foil for wrapping up and heating the prepared bread. Find a small basin, a wooden spoon and a table knife for spreading the butter. Turn on the oven heat to hot (425 °F, 220 °C or Gas No 7).

Using a bread knife slice the Vienna loaves at an angle (so that the slices are a little longer) and almost through the loaf, but not quite, so that you leave the bottom crust whole. Set the bread aside while preparing the herb butter.

And the Small and Sorry Rabbit rushed through the mist at
the noise, and it suddenly turned into Tigger; a Friendly
Tigger, a Grand Tigger, a Large and Helpful Tigger, a Tigger
who bounced, if he bounced at all, in just the beautiful way a
Tigger ought to bounce.
'Oh, Tigger, I am glad to see you,' cried Rabbit.

Put the butter in the basin and beat with a wooden spoon until
soft. Then beat in the lemon juice and the chopped parsley and
chives and mix well.

Spread the butter generously between each slice of bread, taking
care not to break the loaves open too much. Now completely wrap
each buttered loaf in a square of kitchen foil like a parcel.

Put the wrapped bread in the centre of the pre-heated oven and
let it heat through for 20 minutes. Wearing oven gloves, take out,
open the foil and serve the bread at once when it will be crusty and
warm and you can break off the slices. Herb bread is good with
soup, cold meats and salad and very good with omelettes.

Tigger

picnic and 'expotition' foods

Orange sandwiches

———◆———

Cheese scones

———◆———

Rolled oat cookies

———◆———

Apple slices

———◆———

Cut and come again cake

———◆———

Gingerbread

———◆———

Cheese tartlets

Orange Sandwiches

Serves 4

8 slices of brown bread from a large loaf
butter for spreading
3 medium sized oranges
1 teaspoon castor sugar

You will need a cutting board, a sharp kitchen knife and a table knife for spreading the butter. You should also have handy some greaseproof paper and kitchen foil for wrapping if you are going to take the sandwiches on a picnic.

Arrange the slices of brown bread on a cutting board setting them in pairs as they come from the loaf. Butter each one lightly and set aside while preparing the oranges.

He got out of bed and opened his front door.
'Hallo!' said Pooh, in case there was anything outside.
'Hallo!' said Whatever-it-was.

Cut a slice from the top and base of each orange with a sharp
knife. Then stand each orange upright. Cut down round the sides,
following the curve of the orange, to take away the peel and white
pith so that you clean the orange right down to the juicy flesh. You
might find it easier to cut round and round like an apple – it doesn't
matter which way you do it, but I think the first is easier.

Slice the oranges across thinly and remove any pips. Arrange the
orange slices on four of the buttered bread slices and sprinkle them
lightly with sugar. Cover with the remaining four bread slices,
buttered side down, and press gently.

Trim the bread crusts and then cut each sandwich across into two
or four triangles. Wrap the sandwiches in greaseproof paper and in
foil and refrigerate until required. You will find these very refreshing on a picnic.

Cheese Scones

Makes 8 scones

8 oz (or 8 rounded tablespoons) self raising flour

1 level teaspoon baking powder

pinch salt

2 oz butter

2 oz (or 2 heaped tablespoons) grated cheddar cheese

1 egg made up to ¼ pint with milk – about 5 tablespoons

Find a mixing basin, a sieve and a fork for mixing the scones. You will also need a measuring jug, a pastry board and a rolling pin, a kitchen knife and a baking tray. Turn the oven heat to hot (425 °F, 220 °C or Gas No 7) and find a pair of oven gloves.

Sift the flour, baking powder, and salt into the mixing basin. Add the butter and, using finger tips, rub the butter into the sifted flour until evenly mixed with no lumps. Add the grated cheese and mix thoroughly.

'Are these really thistles?' he whispered.
'Yes,' said Pooh.
'What Tiggers like best?'
'That's right,' said Pooh.
'I see,' said Tigger.
So he took a large mouthful, and he gave a large crunch.
'Ow!' said Tigger.

Crack the egg into a measuring jug and make it up to ¼ pint with milk – if you have no measuring jug it is about 5 tablespoons. Mix lightly with a fork.

Pour the egg and milk into the centre of the dry ingredients, and using a fork mix to a rough dough in the basin. Turn on to a floured pastry board and with lightly floured fingers knead the dough for a moment until smooth. Roll the dough out to a square of about ½″ (1 cm) in thickness. Using a floured knife cut the dough into four quarters, then cut each quarter diagonally in half to make eight triangular scones.

Dust the baking tray with flour. Arrange the scones on the tray and dust the scones with flour. Wearing oven gloves, put above centre in the pre-heated oven and bake for 12 minutes.

While still warm, split and butter. For a picnic, top with any sandwich filling or spread them with cream cheese and top with a slice of tomato.

'Do Tiggers like honey?'
'They like everything,'
said Tigger cheerfully.

Rolled Oat Cookies

Makes 24

4 oz (or 4 rounded tablespoons) self raising flour

4 oz (or 8 heaped tablespoons) rolled oats

2 oz white cooking fat

2 oz butter

4 oz (or 4 rounded tablespoons) castor sugar

1 level teaspoon bicarbonate of soda

1 teaspoon golden syrup

1 teaspoon boiling water

These are mixed in the saucepan so find a large sized one and a wooden spoon. You will also need a plate, a sieve, a small basin, a palette knife, a teaspoon for shaping the cookies and a wire cooling tray for when they have baked. Turn the oven heat to moderate (350 °F, 180 °C or Gas No 4) and find a pair of oven gloves. Switch on the kettle for boiling water.

Sift the flour on to a plate, add the rolled oats and set aside. Measure the cooking fat and butter into the saucepan and allow the fat to melt over low heat. Draw the pan off the heat and stir in the sugar.

Measure the bicarbonate of soda, the golden syrup and the boiling water into a small basin. Mix well and stir into the contents of the saucepan. Add the sifted flour and rolled oats and mix well.

Place teaspoonfuls of the mixture on to two greased baking trays – about 12 on each tray. Space the cookies evenly apart for they flatten and spread on baking. Put in the centre of the pre-heated oven and bake for 15–20 minutes. Let cool for a moment and then using a palette knife transfer the cookies to a wire cooling tray. The cookies will become crisp and crunchy as they cool. To keep them crisp put in a lidded tin when quite cold.

Apple Slices

Makes 12 slices

8 oz (or 8 rounded tablespoons) self raising flour
4 oz butter
2 oz (or 2 rounded tablespoons) castor sugar
1 large egg
icing sugar for dusting

For the filling:

1 lb cooking apples
4 oz (or 4 rounded tablespoons) castor sugar
½ level teaspoon ground cinnamon
1 tablespoon seedless raisins

Find one large and two small basins, a plate and a fork. You will also need a pastry board, a rolling pin, a small vegetable knife and a grater. Find a medium sized roasting tin or rectangular baking tin of about 11″×8″ (28 cm×20 cm) and butter it well. Turn on the oven heat to moderate (350 °F, 180 °C or Gas No 4) and find a pair of oven gloves.

Sift the flour into a large mixing basin. Add the butter, cut in pieces, and using finger tips rub the butter into the flour until it is evenly mixed and crumbly. Add the castor sugar and mix thoroughly.

Tigger explained to anybody who was listening that he hadn't
had any breakfast yet.

Lightly mix the egg in a small bowl with a fork. Add this to the
dry ingredients and using the fork mix to a rough dough in the
basin. Turn out on to a floured pastry board and knead for a moment
to get a smooth dough. Then set the prepared pastry aside, under
the upturned mixing bowl, and leave to rest for 30 minutes.

Peel, core and grate the apples on to a plate. In a separate bowl
mix the sugar, cinnamon and raisins.

Divide the pastry dough in half. On a well floured surface roll
out one piece to a rectangle and use to line the base of the buttered
baking tin. Arrange layers of the grated apple and spiced sugar on
the pastry base – start and end with a layer of apple. Roll out the
remaining piece of dough and use it to cover the top.

Set in the centre of the pre-heated oven and bake for 45 minutes
to 1 hour. Remove from the oven and while still warm dust thickly
with icing sugar. Leave until cold. Then cut into 12 slices and lift
out of the tin.

Cut and Come Again Cake

Makes 16 pieces

10 oz (or 10 rounded tablespoons) self raising flour

2 level teaspoons ground mixed spice

1 level teaspoon salt

5 oz butter

5 oz (or 5 rounded tablespoons) soft brown sugar

2 eggs

4 tablespoons milk

1 lb cleaned sultanas

Like all fruit cakes this one keeps well which means you can cut off what you require and come back again for the rest. You will need a large and a small mixing basin, a sieve, a plate, a wooden spoon, a metal spoon and a fork for mixing. Find a medium sized roasting tin or rectangular baking tin of about 11"×8" (28 cm×20 cm) and butter it well. Turn on the oven heat to moderate (350 °F, 180 °C or Gas No 4) and find a pair of oven gloves.

'Tiggers never go on being Sad,' explained Rabbit. 'They get over it with Astonishing Rapidity.'

Sift the flour, mixed spice and salt into the large mixing basin. Add the butter cut in pieces and using the finger tips rub into the flour until evenly mixed and crumbly. Add the sugar, mix and make a well in the centre of the ingredients.

Lightly mix the egg and milk in the small basin. Add all at once to the dry ingredients and using a wooden spoon, stir first to blend the ingredients and then beat thoroughly to mix. Add the sultanas and stir together.

Spoon the mixture into the prepared baking tin and spread level. Place in the centre of the pre-heated oven and bake for 1–1¼ hours or until risen and golden brown. Test by pressing the centre of the cake gently with the fingers – it should feel firm. Let the cake cool in the tin. Then cut what you require into fingers and wrap the remainder in foil or put in a lidded tin to keep.

The mist got thicker, so that Tigger kept disappearing, and then when you thought he wasn't there, there he was again. . . .

Gingerbread

Cuts into 12 pieces

4 oz (or 4 rounded tablespoons) plain flour

pinch salt

½ level teaspoon bicarbonate of soda

1 level teaspoon ground ginger

1 level teaspoon ground cinnamon

2 oz (or two heaped tablespoons) sultanas

1½ oz white cooking fat

2 oz (or 2 rounded tablespoons) soft brown sugar

1 rounded tablespoon golden syrup

1 rounded tablespoon black treacle

1 egg

3 tablespoons milk

You will need both a large and a small mixing basin, a sieve, a wooden spoon, a fork and a saucepan. Find a 7″ (18 cm) shallow square baking tin for the gingerbread, grease it well and line at the bottom with greased greaseproof paper. Turn the oven heat to moderate (350 °F, 180 °C or Gas No 4), find a pair of oven gloves and a wire cooling tray.

Sift the flour, salt, bicarbonate of soda, ginger and cinnamon into a large mixing basin. Add the sultanas. Mix and make a well in the centre.

Put the fat, sugar, syrup and treacle in a saucepan – if you dip a tablespoon in boiling water before measuring the syrup or treacle you will find that it slides off easily. Set the pan over low heat. Stir until the fat has melted and ingredients are blended. Draw the pan off the heat and let the contents cool until just warm.

Using a fork lightly mix the egg and milk together in a small basin. Add the contents of the saucepan and mix very thoroughly with a wooden spoon. Pour into the centre of the dry ingredients and beat well to get a smooth batter.

Pour into the prepared baking tin. Put in the centre of the pre-heated oven and bake for 30 minutes or until the gingerbread is well risen – test by feeling the centre when it should be nice and springy. Turn on to a wire cooling tray and leave until cold. Then cut into pieces.

Gingerbread always tastes best a day or more after it has been baked. Slices of it are also very good spread with butter.

'Thank you, Pooh,' said Tigger, 'because haycorns is really
what Tiggers like best.'
So after breakfast they went round to see Piglet, and Pooh
explained as they went that Piglet was a Very Small Animal
who didn't like bouncing, and asked Tigger not to be too
Bouncy just at first.

Cheese Tartlets

Makes 12

4 oz shortcrust pastry – made using a ready mix or 1 (7½ oz)
packet frozen pastry, thawed

For the filling:

2 eggs
2 tablespoons milk
2 oz (or 2 heaped tablespoons) grated cheddar cheese
salt and freshly milled pepper

You will need a pastry board and a rolling pin, a tray of 12 tartlet
tins and a 2½″ (6 cm) round biscuit cutter. Find a mixing bowl, a
fork and teaspoon. Turn the oven heat to hot (400 °F, 200 °C or
Gas No 6), find a pair of oven gloves and a wire cooling tray.

On a lightly floured pastry board roll out the pastry thinly. Using a round pastry cutter stamp out 12 circles of dough. You may need to knead and re-roll the trimmings to get the last two or three circles. Use the circles to line 12 tartlet tins and set aside in a cool place while preparing the filling.

Crack the eggs into the mixing bowl. Add the milk, the grated cheese and a seasoning of salt and pepper. Mix the ingredients lightly with a fork.

Place teaspoons of the mixture into each pastry-lined case. Place in the centre of the pre-heated oven and bake for 10 minutes. Then lower the oven heat to moderately hot (375 °F, 190 °C or Gas No 5) and bake for a further 5 minutes. When ready the tartlets should be golden brown and puffy. Transfer from the tins on to a wire cooling tray. These cheese tartlets are nice warm or cold.

Kanga and Roo

puddings

Chocolate surprise pudding

———◆———

Pink pears

———◆———

Orange mousse

———◆———

Upside down pineapple cake

———◆———

Orange slices in syrup

———◆———

Fruit fool

'Well,' said Eeyore that afternoon, when he saw them all
walking up to his house, 'this is a surprise.'

Chocolate Surprise Pudding

Serves 4

3 oz (or 3 rounded tablespoons) self raising flour

1 oz (or 2 rounded tablespoons) cocoa powder

pinch salt

4 oz butter or margarine

4 oz (or 4 rounded tablespoons) castor sugar

2 eggs

few drops vanilla essence

1–2 tablespoons milk

For the sauce:

4 oz (or 4 rounded tablespoons) soft brown sugar

1 oz (or 2 rounded tablespoons) cocoa powder

½ pint hot water

You will need a large and a small mixing basin, a sieve, a plate and
a fork, a wooden spoon and a tablespoon. Find a 2-pint baking or
pie dish and butter it well. Set the baking dish on a baking tray
which will make it easier to lift in and out of the oven. Turn the
oven heat to moderately hot (375 °F, 190 °C or Gas No 5) and find
a pair of oven gloves. Fill and switch on the kettle for hot water.

Sift the flour, cocoa powder and salt on to a plate and set aside. Measure the butter and sugar into the large basin and using a wooden spoon beat until creamy.

Lightly mix the eggs and vanilla essence with a fork in a small basin. Gradually beat the egg into the creamed mixture. Add a little of the sifted flour along with the last few additions of egg to prevent the mixture from separating. Fold in the remaining flour with a tablespoon and mix in just enough milk to make a soft consistency. Spoon the cake mixture into the buttered baking dish and spread level.

In the small basin combine the soft brown sugar and cocoa powder. Stir in the hot water and mix well to make a chocolate sauce. Pour this sauce over the cake in the baking dish.

Put the pudding in the centre of the pre-heated oven and bake for 40 minutes. The 'surprise' is that during baking the cake rises to the top and the sauce goes underneath. You have a chocolate pudding with its own delicious chocolate sauce. Serve hot, either with cream or with scoops of vanilla ice cream.

Pink Pears

Serves 6

6 cooking pears

6 oz (or 6 rounded tablespoons) castor sugar

1 pint water

2 pieces of pared lemon rind

juice of ½ lemon

1 small piece of stick cinnamon

2 tablespoons grenadine syrup (or one teaspoon of cochineal) – see below

1 level tablespoon cornflour

You will need a large saucepan with a lid, a vegetable peeler, a wooden spoon, a lemon squeezer, a large and a small mixing basin and a perforated spoon. Find a deep china or earthenware bowl for serving the pears. The cinnamon stick in this recipe can usually be found in a health food store. The grenadine syrup, which turns the pears a beautiful pink, is an orange red syrup made from pomegranates and is stocked by most wine merchants. You can substitute cochineal – a pink food colouring.

Using a vegetable peeler pare away the skins from the pears, leaving them whole. Do not remove the stalks. Put the pears in a bowl of cold water as they are peeled to keep them white, but drain from the water before cooking them.

'Ow!' cried Piglet. 'Let me out! I'm Piglet!'
'Don't open the mouth, dear, or the soap goes in,' said Kanga.

Put the sugar, water, pared lemon rind – use the vegetable peeler for this – the lemon juice, stick cinnamon and grenadine syrup, or the cochineal, in a saucepan. Stir over low heat to dissolve the sugar and then bring up to the boil.

Add the pears to the hot syrup and bring back to a simmer. Cover the pan with a lid and cook gently for 20–30 minutes or until the pears are tender. Test by piercing the pears with a knife when they should feel soft. Draw the pan off the heat.

Using a perforated spoon, lift the pears out and place in the serving dish. Replace the pan of syrup over the heat.

In the small basin blend the cornflour with an extra tablespoon of cold water to make a paste. Stir this into the syrup and keep on stirring until the liquid comes up to the boil and thickens slightly. Strain the syrup over the pears to remove the spices. Leave the pears until quite cold before serving.

By the time they got to Kanga's
house they were so buffeted
that they stayed to lunch.

Orange Mousse

Serves 6

3 medium oranges

1 lemon

4 tablespoons cold water

½ oz (or 1 level tablespoon) powdered gelatine

3 eggs

3 oz (or 3 rounded tablespoons) castor sugar

You will need a large and a medium sized mixing basin, a wooden spoon, a grater, a small saucepan, a lemon squeezer, a metal tablespoon and a whisk for the egg whites. Find a pretty serving bowl for the mousse before you start.

Scrub the oranges and lemon and wipe dry. Then finely grate the rind of 1 orange into the large mixing basin. Cut all the fruits in half, squeeze out the juice and reserve for adding later.

Measure the cold water into the saucepan, sprinkle in the gelatine and let it soak for 5 minutes. Then place over a low heat and stir until the gelatine has dissolved and the liquid is clear – do not allow it to boil. Draw off the heat.

Separate the eggs, putting the yolks in the large basin with the grated orange rind, and the whites in the second mixing basin. Add 2 oz of the sugar to the egg yolks and using a wooden spoon beat well until pale in colour. Stir in the reserved fruit juices.

Discard the wooden spoon and change over to a whisk. Hold the pan of dissolved gelatine well above the mixing basin and pour in a little at a time and whisk so that the gelatine is well blended in. Let the mixture stand in a cool place until it begins to thicken and shows signs of setting – stir occasionally to check; it takes about 10–15 minutes. Wash and dry the whisk for beating the egg whites.

Whisk the egg whites until stiff. Add the rest of the sugar and whisk again until thick and glossy. Using a metal spoon, fold the egg whites gently and evenly into the orange mousse. Pour into a serving bowl and leave in the refrigerator until set firm. You can decorate this pudding with extra segments of orange but they must be peeled free of all pith and membrane.

Upside Down Pineapple Cake

Serves 4–6

2 tablespoons demerara sugar

2 slices of tinned pineapple

few glacé cherries

For the cake mixture:

4 oz (or 4 rounded tablespoons) self raising flour

1 level teaspoon baking powder

3 oz (or 3 rounded tablespoons) castor sugar

3 oz quick creaming margarine

1 egg

2 tablespoons milk

You will need one large and one small mixing bowl, a sieve, a wooden spoon, a fork and a tablespoon. To bake the pudding you will need a 1½ pint round glass ovenware dish (which looks best) or you could use an oval pie dish of the same size. Generously grease the baking dish (especially over the base) and find a baking tray to set it on. Turn the oven heat to moderately hot (375 °F, 190 °C or Gas No 5) and find a pair of oven gloves.

Sprinkle the insides of the buttered dish with the demerara sugar – take care to get a good layer on the base otherwise the decoration will stick when you come to turn the pudding out. Arrange a pattern in the base using the cut up pineapple and a few pieces of glacé cherry. Set aside while preparing the cake mixture.

Sift the flour and baking powder into the large mixing bowl. Add the margarine and the sugar. In a small bowl lightly mix the egg and milk with a fork. Add to the dry ingredients and using a wooden spoon stir first to blend the ingredients and then beat thoroughly for 1 minute to get a smooth cake batter.

Spoon the cake batter carefully into the prepared baking dish, taking care not to disturb the decoration of fruit. Spread the mixture level.

Set the dish on a baking tray. Put in the centre of the pre-heated oven and bake for 30 minutes. To serve put a serving plate over the pudding and invert so that it falls out on to the plate with the decoration on top. Serve hot with cream.

It was the first party to which Roo
had ever been, and he was very excited.

Orange Slices in Syrup

Serves 6

6 medium oranges

6 oz (or 6 rounded tablespoons) castor sugar

¼ pint water

juice of ½ lemon

You will need a large mixing basin in which to blanch the oranges.
Find a chopping board, a sharp kitchen knife, a lemon squeezer, a
saucepan and a wooden spoon. Choose a pretty serving dish for the
oranges and set it beside you. Switch on the kettle for boiling water.

Using a small knife mark the rind of each orange into quarters as
if you were going to peel them. Put the oranges all together in a
large bowl and cover with boiling water. Let them stand for 5
minutes so that the peel softens.

Drain off the water and while the oranges are still hot, pull away the peel. You will find that most of the white pith comes off as well – any that remains can easily be scraped off with a knife – so that you clean the oranges right down to the fine membrane that covers the juicy flesh.

Using a sharp knife cut the oranges across into thin slices. Discard any pips and arrange the slices in the serving bowl. Set aside while you prepare the syrup.

Measure the sugar and water into the saucepan. Set over low heat and stir to dissolve the sugar. Then bring up to the boil and simmer for 1 minute. Draw the pan off the heat.

Add the juice of the lemon and pour the hot syrup over the orange slices. Cool and then chill the oranges until they are really cold. These are delicious with vanilla ice cream.

Fruit Fool

Serves 4

1 lb fresh fruit or canned fruit – gooseberries, apricots, blackcurrants or rhubarb

3–4 oz (or 3–4 rounded tablespoons) castor sugar – see below

½ oz (or 1 level tablespoon) custard powder

1 level tablespoon castor sugar

½ pint milk

You will need a medium sized saucepan for cooking the fruit and making the custard. Find 2 mixing basins and a wooden spoon. For serving you will need 4 individual glass dishes.

Prepare fresh fruits according to the kind chosen. Put in a saucepan with about 2 tablespoons cold water. Set over low heat and bring to a simmer. Cover and cook for about 5–10 minutes or until the fruit is quite soft. Draw off the heat and add the sugar. Stir until the sugar has dissolved, then pass the fruit and juices through a sieve set over a basin to make a purée. Let the purée cool.

```
         this                    take
'If    is        shall      really      to
       flying I        never                it.'
```

Where tinned fruits are used there is no need to cook or sweeten the fruit mixture. Press the fruits and about 3 tablespoons of the syrup through a sieve or blend in a liquidizer to make a purée. Set the fruit aside while preparing the custard. Rinse out the saucepan.

Measure the custard powder and the remaining tablespoon of sugar into a small mixing bowl. Add 3 tablespoons of the milk and mix ingredients to a thin paste. Pour the rest of the milk into a saucepan and set over low heat. Stir the hot milk into the custard blend. Mix well and return to the milk saucepan.

Replace the pan over the heat and cook stirring all the time until the custard has thickened and is boiling. Pour into a mixing basin and leave to cool, stirring occasionally to prevent a skin forming.

Add the custard to the fruit purée and stir to blend. Mix thoroughly for a creamy consistency. Taste for sweetness and then pour into individual serving glasses. Chill for several hours before serving. For a party you can sprinkle these with toasted flaked almonds and serve with sponge finger biscuits.

Christopher Robin
cold drinks and ices

Honey banana milk shake

———◆———

Vanilla ice cream

———◆———

Lemon and orange fruit cup

———◆———

Baked Alaska

———◆———

Liquidizer lemonade

———◆———

Orange water ice

Here is Edward Bear, coming downstairs now, bump, bump,
bump, on the back of his head, behind Christopher Robin

Honey Banana Milk Shake

Makes 2 long drinks
1 fully ripe banana
½ pint chilled milk
1 tablespoon clear honey
1 scoopful vanilla ice cream

You will need an electric liquidizer or a rotary hand whisk, a
measuring jug and a knife. Find two tall tumblers and some straws
for serving.

It's best to make milk shakes in a liquidizer if you can because
they come up beautifully frothy. Make sure the machine is switched
off before you start. Or you can beat the sliced banana, honey and
ice cream in a bowl with a rotary hand whisk before adding the
milk.

Peel and cut the banana into the liquidizer goblet. Pour in the
chilled milk and add the honey and ice cream. Cover and blend on
low speed to mix, then froth up on high speed for a few seconds.

Pour into tall glasses and serve with straws.

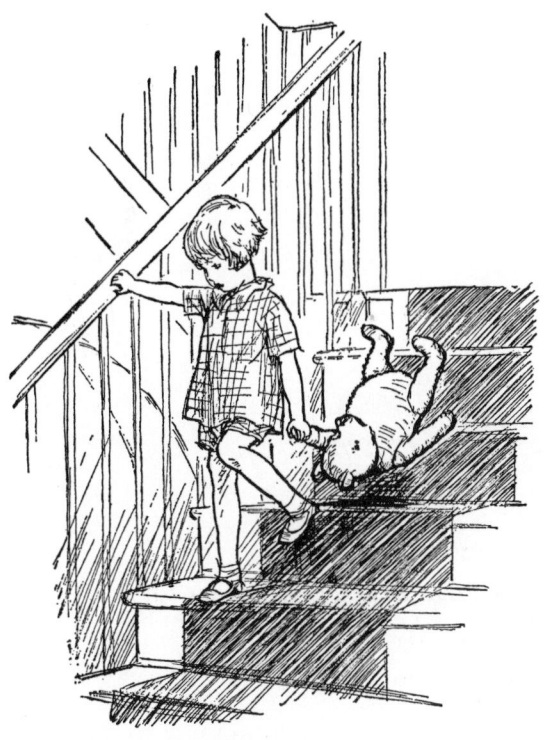

Vanilla Ice Cream

Serves 6

3 eggs

4 oz (or 4 rounded tablespoons) castor sugar

few drops vanilla essence

½ pint double cream

You will need 1 large and 2 medium-sized basins, a wooden spoon, a whisk and a tablespoon. For freezing the ice cream find a polythene refrigerator container of about 2½ pints capacity with a fitting lid.

Separate the eggs, putting the yolks into the large mixing basin and the whites into one of the medium-sized basins. Pour the cream into the third basin. Add half the sugar and the vanilla essence to the egg yolks and, using a wooden spoon, mix very thoroughly.

Whisk the egg whites until stiff. Sprinkle in the rest of the sugar and whisk again until glossy. Whisk the cream until it stands in soft peaks.

'One of those big coloured things you blow up? Gaiety,
song-and-dance, here we are and there we are?'

Add the beaten egg whites and the whipped cream to the egg
yolk mixture and using a metal spoon fold all the ingredients gently
but thoroughly together. Pour the mixture into a suitable container,
cover and put in the freezer. Leave for about 6 hours or overnight
until firm.

To serve, transfer the ice cream container to the refrigerator for
30 minutes and you will find it scoops out beautifully.

Two ice cream sodas
If you like ice cream sodas try these two ideas. Put a scoop of vanilla
ice cream in a tall tumbler and top up with ginger beer. Or do the
same and top up with Coca Cola. Serve with straws for drinking and
a spoon to scoop out the ice cream.

Lemon and Orange Fruit Cup

Serves 12 glasses

2 lemons

4 oz (or 4 rounded tablespoons) castor sugar

1 pint water

1 pint orange juice – canned or frozen reconstituted

1 pint ginger ale

slices of orange for garnish

Find a chopping board, a kitchen knife and a saucepan. You will also need a large basin, a wooden spoon, a lemon squeezer and a strainer. Select a tall glass jug for serving the fruit cup.

Wash the lemons and wipe them dry. Cut each one in half and squeeze out the juice. Reserve the lemon juice for adding later and put the lemon peel in the large mixing basin.

Add the sugar to the lemon peels. Bring the water to the boil in a saucepan and pour over the sugar and lemon peels. Stir with a wooden spoon to dissolve the sugar. Leave until quite cold.

Strain the lemon mixture into the tall serving jug. Add the lemon and orange juices and put in the refrigerator to chill. When ready to serve, stir in the ginger ale and add a few slices of orange for garnish.

Pour into ice-filled tumblers – you can add the slices of orange (cut in half) to each glass if you prefer.

Suddenly Christopher Robin began to laugh . . . and he laughed . . .
and he laughed . . . and he laughed. And while he was still laughing –
Crash went the Heffalump's head against the tree-root, Smash went
the jar, and out came Pooh's head again.

Baked Alaska

Serves 6

1 baked sponge flan
1 tablespoon raspberry jam
1 (300 ml or 10·4 fl oz) brick of vanilla ice cream

For the meringue:
3 egg whites
6 oz (or 6 rounded tablespoons) castor sugar

You will need an oven proof baking dish or plate on which to set the sponge flan for baking and serving. You will also need a table-spoon, a large basin and a whisk for the meringue. Turn the oven heat to hot (425 °F, 220 °C or Gas No 7) and find a pair of oven gloves.

This is the kind of recipe you make up and serve at once so have everything ready before you start. Spread the inside of the sponge flan with the jam and set on the oven proof serving plate. Put the egg whites in the large basin and have the sugar ready.

And when he had finished laughing, they all sang the
Outdoor Song for Snowy Weather.

Whisk the egg whites until stiff and standing in peaks. Add one
third of the sugar and whisk again until glossy. Add the second
third of sugar and whisk until stiff. Fold in the last third of sugar
carefully using a metal spoon. Unwrap the vanilla ice cream and
place in the sponge flan.

Pile the meringue on top of the ice cream and using a spoon swirl
it down the sides and around the ice cream and sponge to enclose
both completely This insulates the ice cream from the heat of the
oven.

Put the Alaska in the centre of the pre-heated oven and bake for
2–3 minutes or until the meringue is just golden. Serve at once,
cutting into it like a cake. The meringue will be hot but inside the
ice cream will be quite cold.

For a long time they looked at the river beneath them, saying nothing, and the river said nothing too, for it felt very quiet and peaceful on this summer afternoon.

Liquidizer Lemonade

Serves 3 long drinks

2 lemons

4 oz (or 4 rounded tablespoons) castor sugar

water – see below

This is a most refreshing lemon drink to make on a liquidizer attachment or one of the free standing models. To make this recipe it has to be one of the larger 2 pint capacity machines. Check that the machine is switched off at the wall before starting. All you need is a chopping board, a knife, a strainer and 3 tall glasses. Put a few lumps of ice in each glass and you are ready to go.

Cut the lemons into chunky pieces including skin and pips. Place in the liquidizer goblet and add the sugar.

Fill the goblet up to the 1½ pint level. Cover with the lid. Switch the machine on high and blend for a few minutes or until the lemons are very finely chopped.

Strain into the ice-filled tumblers and serve.

Mixed fruit drink

You can make a *mixed fruit drink* by cutting up 1 orange and 1 lemon in the same way. You will need less sugar – only 2 oz (or 2 rounded tablespoons) – and the same amount of water.

'I like that too,' said Christopher Robin,
'but what I like doing best is Nothing.'

Orange Water Ice

Serves 6

½ pint cold water

2 level teaspoons powdered gelatine

6 oz (or 6 rounded tablespoons) castor sugar

1 (6¼ oz) carton frozen concentrated orange juice

2 egg whites

Find a small mixing basin or cup, a saucepan and a wooden spoon. For freezing the water ice you will need a polythene refrigerator container of about 1½ pints capacity with a fitting lid. For whisking the water ice at a later stage you should have ready 2 medium-sized mixing basins and a whisk.

Measure 2 tablespoons of the water into a small mixing basin or cup and sprinkle in the gelatine. Let soak for 5 minutes.

Pour the rest of the water into a saucepan and add the sugar. Set over low heat and stir until the sugar has dissolved. Bring up to the boil and simmer for 1 minute, then draw the pan off the heat.

Add the soaked gelatine and stir until dissolved – the heat of the pan will be sufficient to do this. Then add the undiluted orange juice concentrate – it can be added while still frozen. Stir to blend and leave until quite cold.

Pour the orange mixture into a suitable container and freeze until mushy – about 2 hours.

Put the egg white in a medium-sized mixing basin and whisk until stiff. Turn the half-frozen water ice into the second basin and whisk until smooth. Then whisk the egg white into the water ice and mix thoroughly. Immediately pour the mixture back into the container, cover and refreeze for several hours or until firm.

This will make sufficient orange water ice to scoop into 6 sundae glasses – it tastes very fresh and cool. You can follow the recipe using a can of frozen, concentrated grapefruit juice to make a grapefruit water ice in exactly the same way.

Eeyore
soups and vegetable dishes

Watercress soup

———◆———

Scalloped potatoes

———◆———

Ratatouille with cheese

———◆———

Corn fritters

———◆———

Lentil soup with croutons

'Oh, Eeyore, you **are** wet!' said Piglet, feeling him. Eeyore shook
himself, and asked somebody to explain to Piglet what happened
when you had been inside a river for a very long time.

Watercress Soup

Serves 6

2 bunches watercress

1 oz butter

1 medium onion

1 lb potatoes

1½ pints chicken stock (made using 2 chicken cubes and water)

½ pint milk

salt and freshly milled pepper

You will need a chopping board and a kitchen knife, a saucepan and
a wooden spoon. To purée the soup a liquidizer is best or you can
use a Mouli soup mill or a sieve set over a large mixing basin.

Wash both bunches of watercress in cold water. Nip the leaves
off one bunch and set aside for the garnish. Trim and chop up the
remaining leaves and the stalks of both bunches. Peel and chop the
onion and peel and cut the potatoes into dice.

Melt the butter in a medium-sized saucepan. Add the chopped onion, diced potatoes and chopped watercress. Cover and cook very gently for a few minutes to soften the vegetables.

Stir in the chicken stock and bring up to a simmer. Cover and cook for 15–20 minutes or until the potatoes are quite soft. Draw off the heat and add the milk to the pan.

Purée the liquid and vegetables in an electric liquidizer or pass through a soup mill or sieve. Check the seasoning and add salt and pepper if necessary. Finely chop the reserved watercress and add. Return the soup to the pan. Re-heat for serving but do not boil.

'It's Eeyore!' cried Roo, terribly excited.
'Is that so?' said Eeyore, getting caught up by a little eddy,
and turning slowly round three times. 'I wondered.'

Scalloped Potatoes

Serves 4

1½ lbs potatoes

1 large onion

salt and freshly milled pepper

1½ oz butter

1 oz (or 1 rounded tablespoon) plain flour

¾ pint milk

2 oz (or 2 heaped tablespoons) grated cheddar cheese

Find a chopping board, a kitchen knife, a vegetable peeler and a saucepan in which to blanch the potatoes and make the sauce. You will also need a wooden spoon, a colander and a measuring jug. For baking the scalloped potatoes you will need a buttered paper or square of kitchen foil and a baking dish of about 1½–2 pints capacity. Butter the dish thoroughly. Turn on the oven heat to low (300 °F, 150 °C or Gas No 2) and find a pair of oven gloves.

Wash and peel the potatoes and cut them into ¼ inch thick slices. Put these in the saucepan, cover with cold water and bring to the boil. Simmer for no more than 4 minutes to blanch them, and then drain in a colander. Peel and chop the onion.

Arrange alternate layers of potato slices and chopped onion in a well buttered baking dish and season each layer with salt and pepper. Add about ½ oz butter in flakes. Set aside while preparing the sauce.

Melt the remaining butter in the rinsed saucepan and add the flour. Stir with a wooden spoon over low heat for a moment. Then gradually stir in the milk, beating well all the time to get a smooth sauce. Bring up to a simmer and cook for 1–2 minutes. Season to taste with salt and pepper and add half the grated cheese.

Pour the sauce over the potato slices. Cover with a buttered paper or foil, put the potatoes in the pre-heated oven and bake for about 2 hours.

When the potatoes are ready they will feel quite tender if you pierce them with a knife. Sprinkle with the remaining cheese and put the dish under a hot grill to brown the topping. Serve hot – these are very nice with something plain like cold roast chicken.

Ratatouille with Cheese

Serves 4

1 lb courgettes

4 large onions

2 tablespoons oil

1 (15 oz) tin tomatoes

salt and freshly milled pepper

1 level teaspoon castor sugar

1 bay leaf

1 tablespoon chopped parsley

2–3 oz (or 2–3 heaped tablespoons) grated cheddar cheese

Ratatouille is a delicious vegetable stew. To make it you will need a chopping board, a kitchen knife, a vegetable peeler and a can opener. Find a medium-sized frying pan with a lid for cooking the ratatouille and put a dish for serving to warm.

'Nobody tells me,' said Eeyore. 'Nobody keeps me informed. I make it seventeen days come Friday since anybody spoke to me.'

Wash the courgettes, trim them and then slice about ½ inch (1 cm) thick. Peel and slice the onions.

Heat the oil in a medium-sized frying pan and add the onions. Keep the heat low and very gently fry the onions for about 5 minutes or until they have softened. Add the courgettes, the tomatoes along with the juice from the tin, a seasoning of salt and pepper, the sugar (this counteracts the acid taste of the tomatoes) and the bay leaf. Cover the pan with a lid and let the vegetables simmer gently for 30 minutes.

Remove the pan lid towards the end of the cooking time to allow any excess liquid to evaporate. Discard the bay leaf and transfer the ratatouille to a warm serving dish. Sprinkle with the parsley and serve the grated cheese separately. Each person should sprinkle his own cheese. Ratatouille is nice with crusty bread, or you can serve it with something plain like an omelette.

'Very interesting,' said Eeyore. 'I suppose they will be sending me down the odd bits which got trodden on. Kind and Thoughtful. Not at all, don't mention it.'

Corn Fritters

Makes 12 fritters

3 oz (or 3 rounded tablespoons) self raising flour

1 egg

2 tablespoons milk

2 tablespoons water

1 (11 oz) can creamed sweetcorn

salt and freshly milled pepper

2 oz butter

1 tablespoon oil

Find a medium-sized mixing basin, a wooden spoon and a tablespoon. You will also need a frying pan, a fish slice and a plate with a little crumpled absorbent kitchen paper for draining the corn fritters. Put a serving plate to warm.

Sift the flour into the mixing basin and make a well in the centre. To the well in the flour add the egg, milk and water. Using a wooden spoon gradually mix the ingredients, keeping the liquid in the centre of the bowl but gradually drawing in the flour from around the sides. Then beat very well to get a smooth batter. Add the creamed sweetcorn and a seasoning of salt and pepper and mix well.

Heat the butter and oil in a frying pan. Drop tablespoons of the corn batter into the hot pan – not more than about four at a time. Cook them gently for 3–4 minutes and turn each one with a fish slice to brown both sides.

Lift the fritters from the pan and drain on the absorbent kitchen paper. Keep warm while frying the rest of the batter. You should get about 12 fritters in all. Serve three corn fritters per person – they are delicious with grilled bacon.

Lentil Soup with Croutons

Serves 6

1 oz butter

1 medium onion or leek

2–3 carrots

2 medium potatoes

6 oz lentils

2½ pints stock (made using 2 chicken cubes and water)

1 bay leaf

salt and freshly milled pepper

For the croutons:

3 slices white bread

1 oz butter

You will need a chopping board, a kitchen knife, a vegetable peeler, a measuring jug and a good sized saucepan with a lid. To purée the soup a liquidizer is best, or you can use a soup mill or a sieve set over a large basin. You will also need a frying pan and a palette knife for the croutons and a bowl in which to serve them. There is no need to soak lentils beforehand.

'It's a Useful Pot,' said Pooh. 'Here it is. And it's got 'A
Very Happy Birthday with love from Pooh' written on it.
That's what all that writing is. And it's for putting things in.
There!'

Melt the butter in the large saucepan. Peel and chop the onion
and peel and dice the carrots and potatoes. Add the vegetables to
the hot butter and fry gently for a few moments to soften them.
Add the lentils.

Gradually stir in the stock, add the bay leaf and bring to a
simmer. Skim and then cover the pan with a lid. Cook the soup
gently for 45 minutes or until the lentils are tender. To check scoop
out a lentil and squeeze between the fingers. Draw off the heat and
discard the bay leaf.

Purée the liquid and vegetables in an electric liquidizer or pass
through a soup mill or sieve. Taste to make sure that the seasoning
with salt and pepper is right. Return the soup to the pan and re-
heat.

Meanwhile trim the crusts from the bread slices and cut into
small dice. Melt the butter in a small frying pan and when hot add
the diced bread cubes. Fry fairly quickly, turning them often with
a palette knife until they are crisp and brown. Pile into a serving
dish and pass this round for guests to help themselves to a sprinkle
of croutons.

Metric conversion table

The following list shows the Imperial measures used in the recipes in this book and their equivalent metric measures balanced to the nearest 5 grammes. If you prefer to work with metric measures you may like to use these as a guide.

Dry Measures		Liquid Measures	
½ oz	15 g	¼ teaspoon	1.25 ml
1 oz	25 g	½ teaspoon	2.5 ml
2 oz	50 g	1 teaspoon	5 ml
3 oz	75 g	1 dessertspoon	10 ml
4 oz	100 g	1 tablespoon	15 ml
5 oz	125 g	1 fl. oz	25 ml
6 oz	150 g	2 fl. oz	50 ml
7 oz	175 g	4 fl. oz	100 ml
8 oz	200 g	¼ pint (5 fl. oz)	125 ml
9 oz	225 g	½ pint (10 fl. oz)	250 ml
	(¼ kilo)		(¼ litre)
10 oz	250 g	¾ pint (15 fl. oz)	375 ml
11 oz	275 g	1 pint (20 fl. oz)	500 ml
12 oz	300 g		(½ litre)
13 oz	325 g		
14 oz	350 g		
15 oz	375 g		
16 oz	400 g		

Index